HOW TO WIN ARGUMENTS WITHOUT ARGUING:
SOCRATIC JUJITSU

BY JENNIFER HANCOCK

Published by Jennifer Hancock
Copyright 2017 by Jennifer Hancock
Published 2017

ISBN-13: 978-1979091855
ISBN-10: 1979091854

This book is also available in digital ebook format

Discover other titles by Jennifer Hancock at:
http://www.jen-hancock.com/

Take the online course at:
https://humanistlearning.com/socratic-jujitsu/

All rights reserved. No part of this book may be used or reproduced in any manner whatsoever without written permission, except in the case of brief quotations embodied in critical articles or reviews.

~~~~~

Table of Contents

Introduction ...5

How to Employ Socratic Jujitsu ...9

Yielding to Disarm ...11

Framing the Conversation ...15

Framing the Conversation in Practice ...19

Collaborative Problem Solving ...23

Freethought ...29

Conclusion ...30

About the Author ...31

CHAPTER 1: INTRODUCTION

Why this Book

This is the companion book to the online course: "How to Win Arguments Without Arguing: Socratic Jujitsu" created by Jennifer Hancock for Humanist Learning Systems. This book contains the transcripts of the online lessons compiled for easy home reference.

The online version of this course contains over 1 hour of video lessons covering recent research on how ideas are formed and changed to help you learn how to persuade people to your point of view more effectively. Understanding why and how to turn conversations around using Socratic questioning techniques will help you frame the underlying moral debate to your advantage.

The online course is facilitated and participants can ask questions and receive feedback directly from Jennifer Hancock. Learn more or register at: https://humanistlearning.com

Introduction

How does one win an argument by not arguing? We employ a technique that I like to call Socratic Jujitsu. Jujitsu as a martial art is soft and yielding. The art of jujitsu is to use your opponent's force and strength against them by yielding.

The idea that you can yield and still "win" is a bit bizarre for most people, because yielding is seen as a weakness

Except that it isn't.

Why Yielding is Not Weak

Master John Chung Li brought Hwa Yu tai chi to America in the 1970s. He taught my master Robert Xavier, who I have studied under since 2012. Most people know Tai Chi as the exercise old people do in parks, but it's actually a martial art. In Tai Chi, you never are the aggressor and you win by not fighting. For this reason, the fights are over very quickly, and there are few images of Tai Chi in use as a martial art.

When someone fights using Tai Chi, the opponent comes at them, and then the aggressor is on the ground. The masters don't even break a sweat. John Li would say, "At my slightest touch, I send my opponent flying."

He didn't use strength, he used the momentum of the other person against them and directed that momentum where he wanted it to go.

He and the other masters could do this because they perfected the art of yielding. They don't fight. They simply aid the other person in defeating themselves.

The Tai Chi master isn't fighting. They are disabling aggression. You disable aggression, not by allowing the other person to attack you, but by allowing them to attempt to attack you and fail. You get out of their way, and sometimes direct them face first to the floor with love and a smile on your face. Always with a smile on your face.

How to Apply the Principals of Tai Chi to Winning Moral Arguments

The first step of winning a moral argument by yielding is not to fight. We aren't going to try and convince our opponent that we are right and they are wrong. We aren't going to try and convince them that our way is better. We are not even going to debate them. That is fighting.

We don't want to fight stupidity with more stupidity.

If we fight, our opponent will dig in their heels and refuse to accept our premise. We may be right, but we will not have won the argument. To win, we have to actually get our opponent to agree with us. To do this we are going to focus on how to solve the problem that is at the heart of the debate. Then we will help walk our opponent through our reasoning step by step until they reach our conclusion.

You will only convince them to see your point of view if you foster inquiry into THEIR reasoning first.

CHAPTER 2: HOW TO EMPLOY SOCRATIC JUJITSU

This is a quick overview of how to win arguments without arguing. We will go into each of these points in more detail later.

1) **Yield** – concede their point – Even if the other person's premise is complete nonsense, conditionally accept it. By doing this you not only show respect, you also disarm them. You have signaled, you aren't going to fight them and most people will lower their defenses and allow a discussion to occur at this point.

2) **Frame the problem** or conversation in moral terms everyone can agree with.

3) **Use Socratic questioning** to help problem solve together. This is not adversarial – it's collaborative. Our goal is to solve the problem, or rather to have them explain to us why their ideas would or would not solve the problem.

If their ideas are complete nonsense, they will figure that out without us having to challenge them or tell them so outright. We are inviting them to convince us that they are right. By allowing them to explain their reasoning to us, they discover for themselves the flaws in their argument.

It has been known for decades that most people have a superficial understanding of the opinions they hold. They have an opinion. They think they know why they hold that opinion. But the reality is – their opinion is based on shallow knowledge. This applies to everyone as no one can be an expert in everything.

It is only when we are asked to explain how something works that we realize how little we understood it. For more information on this, please see http://mindhacks.com/2014/05/26/the-best-way-to-win-an-argument/

Recently, Philip Fernbach, of the University of Colorado tested to see whether helping people realize how superficial their knowledge really is can help them change their minds. He tested this using contentious political issues with his subjects and his conclusion was that yes, realizing they had a shallow understanding of a subject did help people change their minds even on divisive issues. See http://scholar.harvard.edu/files/todd_rogers/files/political_extremism.pdf for more information on this study

We may still agree to disagree at the end, but we will have probably made more headway in encouraging our opponent to question their own beliefs, values, and ideas than if we attacked them and told them that they are stupid.

~~~~~

CHAPTER 3: YIELDING TO DISARM

Normally when an argument starts, our opponent says something we disagree with. We tell them we disagree and start to explain why our opponent is wrong, all while they are trying to tell us why we are wrong.

But what would happen if you didn't argue?

The Framework of an Argument

An argument is made up of premises and a conclusion. A premise is an assertion of fact. If the premises are true and the logic is good, there is a good probability that our conclusion is good too.

As an example, let's use an argument we know is false. All flowers are animals. all animals can jump. Therefore, all flowers can jump.

In this example, the premises are false but the logic is good. The conclusion is false even though the logic is good because the premises are false.

We can also have arguments where the initial premise is correct, and the conclusion is basically correct, but the second premise is faulty.

For example: A cat is an animal. All animals can jump. Therefore, all cats can jump. When considering logic, we need to understand, premises can be false and conclusions may not follow or be logical even though the conclusion is true.

Finally, their premises may be true but the logic may be bad. People who have their facts straight, don't always make logical arguments. It is possible for premises to be true and the conclusion to not follow logically from the premises.

For a conclusion to be considered valid, the premises must be true and the logic must be good. This is why critical thinkers spend time learning about logical fallacies.

When we have an argument with someone, it's usually because we don't agree with their conclusion. There are several ways we can "argue" with them. We can argue that their premises aren't true or that there is a problem with their logic. However, most arguments are almost always about whether the premises are true so that we can disregard the conclusion.

Arguing premises rarely works. In the case of divisive issues like abortion and climate change, opponents get stuck on questions of whether a fetus is a child or whether climate change is caused by humans. These arguments ultimately go nowhere because we are arguing premises and not conclusions. Arguing premises is also not very rational.

To win arguments without arguing, we are not going attack our opponent's premises, instead is we are going to yield. We are going to accept their premises tentatively and conditionally, but not their conclusion. Even if we know their premises are false, we are going to accept them conditionally by saying, "Let's assume this is true."

You yield without conceding.

Yielding without conceding is how you disarm your opponent. There is no argument anymore.

There is now a one-sided discussion. They have to convince you their argument is valid. You aren't trying to convince them of anything. And because you aren't, they are thrown off balance. They were expecting a fight that didn't materialize. You aren't forcing them to listen to or consider your arguments. You aren't even offering yours. You are simply giving them an opportunity to justify their position to you.

As they defend their reasoning, you are going to use Socratic questioning to see if they can convince you to change your mind. You don't do this to win, but because YOU are willing to change YOUR mind. At least I hope you are. You should be sincere in wanting to hear what your opponent has to say or this won't work.

If you are using these techniques to win arguments, you won't learn anything.

A Humanist is willing to change their mind and to have their assumptions challenged. Use these arguments as opportunities to have your assumptions challenged. You may learn something. You may only learn how people rationalize nonsense, but that's still something worth learning. If you listen, you might find that their reasons aren't as crazy as you thought, you just hadn't considered it from another point of view before.

Every time you concede a point, you disarm your opponent and positively incline them towards you as a rational person capable of being reasoned with. When you ask questions that challenge their assumptions, they will likely reciprocate that respect. Why? Because you are modelling the behavior you want them to exhibit. You are creating a mind changing norm. They would look like idiots to not concede your points after you concede theirs. What normally ends up happening when you ask them questions to learn from them, is that you end up walking them through why their argument doesn't work, even if their premises are valid.

~~~~~

CHAPTER 4: FRAMING THE CONVERSATION

Once we have disarmed our opponent, we now need to agree upon what a moral outcome is by framing the conversation we are having. Presumably if we are arguing, it is about something important. That something is usually a problem that needs to be solved and we have competing ideas on how best to solve it. Instead of arguing about which proposal is better, we are going to engage in a discussion about what it is we are ideally trying to accomplish.

We can't discuss which proposal is better until we agree on the ideal outcome. Don't assume there is agreement on what an ideal outcome is. Discuss is and see if you can agree.

It is important to frame the conversation and gain agreement on what a good outcome is before we proceed. In my experience, the first person to put forth a moral framework wins.

What is a frame?

A frame is the moral imperative upon which we are going to decide whether any particular solution is good or not

Framing is all about morality. It involves asking why does this subject matter? What is it that we ideally hope will happen?

By framing a conversation, we do two things. We are getting our first point of agreement, our first yes.

Second, we define what a solution that accomplishes both of our objectives looks like. Third, we take the topics we can't agree on off the table and focus on those we can. This will again, disarm our opponent and force them into the conversation we want to have.

If they agree with us on what the ideal outcome is, they can no longer argue with us. We are now engaged in a cooperative discussion on how best to accomplish the objectives they themselves defined. To do this, we accept their premises or at least the morality underlying their premises. You cannot do that if you assume you know what is motivating them.

When you assume, you argue a strawman. A strawman is the bad argument you think the other person has, but it isn't a real argument held by anyone. It's the fake argument you want to believe people think and not what they actually think. To find that out what is really motivating the other person, you need to ask them questions and accept their answers at face value.

You do not argue with them, you listen to them!

Examples of Moral Framing in Debate

Abortion – this is about limiting or reducing the number of abortions. Something most people can agree on.

Death Penalty -- this is about preventing murders. Right?

Prayer in Schools -- this is about religious freedom.

Racial Profiling by Police -- this is about keeping communities safe.

The point of agreeing on a moral frame of reference is so that you can agree on what a good outcome is. Then you can then discuss how best to accomplish that outcome

~~~

CHAPTER 5: FRAMING THE CONVERSATION IN PRACTICE

Let's look at some very real debates we have about public policy in America so we can see how we frame conversations and debates versus how we should ideally frame them so that we can resolve these debates.

Abortion. One side argues that abortion is bad. It is the killing of a child. It's morally horrid. That is their moral frame. The other side argues that abortion is a necessary choice. That the benefits of allowing women to choose when or if to have a family is so great that we need to give women that choice and that autonomy.

If you are on the choice side, there are several moral frames you can promote: individual autonomy, access to health care as a human right, economic benefits to society, etc..

None of the moral frames surrounding choice are compelling. Someone who thinks abortion is evil and the killing of a child is never going to value individual autonomy over the death of a child. Never! In fact, they take that moral frame and use it to support their point, killing an autonomous individual child is bad!

But what if the pro-choice side accepted the moral framework of their opponent, that abortions are bad? I accept that premise. Everyone should be able to accept that premise. Abortions are bad. They are the killing of a child. We no longer have to debate that.

Let's all agree we should limit abortions. The big question is how?

Notice what just happened. We had been debating, "Are abortions bad?"

But if we accept the premise that abortions *are* bad, and the conclusion that comes with it, that we should limit the number of abortions, we take that debate off the table. It's no longer up for discussion. We have agreed on it.

We have changed the frame of the conversation from whether or not abortions are bad into how can we best prevent abortions. Preventing abortions is something that pretty much everyone can agree on.

It is through the discussion of how best reduce the number of abortions that the punitive approach – make it illegal - falls apart. It doesn't work to reduce or eliminate abortions. It doesn't produce the outcome the anti-choice people want.

What are our other options then? It is at this point that we can now have a productive discussion.

Another example of an emotionally divisive topic is **the death penalty**. One side argues it is necessary to prevent further violent crime. The other side argues it's a human rights violation that does nothing to prevent future violent crime. We are stuck arguing something with no way to resolve the dispute. And no – statistics don't help.

But what if instead of arguing whether or not the death penalty is effective, we start by agreeing with the moral frame of wanting to prevent future violent crime? Now we can discuss the variety of ways that we might be able to do that and we can consider the death penalty as one of many possible alternatives to how we might reduce the rate of violent crime.

We've changed the frame and what it is we are debating about. We aren't debating the death penalty. We are yielding to the underlying moral premise. Murder is bad, so let's figure out a way to reduce it.

~~~~

CHAPTER 6: COLLABORATIVE PROBLEM SOLVING

To recap up to this point:

We have refused to argue by yielding. We can only yield AFTER we learn what the other person really thinks and why they think that, and this requires us to ask questions.

This is why we call this Socratic Jujitsu.

Do NOT assume you know what they think. If you do you will end up arguing a strawman.

To learn what they actually think, we have to ask them questions.

By yielding, we have reframed the conversation based on the moral framework our opponent holds and we found out what our opponent actually wants by asking the following questions: Why? Why do you think this is important? What is it you hope comes out of your policy proposal?

We have accepted their moral premise and what it is they want to accomplish as being morally good.

So far it seems like the other person is winning, right?

Wrong.

All we have done to this point is figure out what it is they want to accomplish and more importantly, why they want to accomplish it. Now we are going to engage in further Socratic questioning with the goal to collaboratively solve the problem our friend has presented and figure out a solution that might actually solve the problem in a way we can all agree on.

When you focus the conversation on how solutions can actually be implemented an interesting thing happens. The conversation stops being a competition and starts being a collaboration. To do this well, you should be Socratic, meaning, you have to get yourself out of the way and allow the other person to do the thinking and the reasoning.

Do not rob them of the empowering experience of flexing their logic muscles by forcing your ideas on them. If there is a flaw in their reasoning, it will be uncovered through the questioning. They will discover the flaw if you ask them questions. And what you want is for them to discover the problem for themselves.

I always enter these conversations with the goal to learn in mind. Maybe they know something I don't. I try and find out what that may be. If they state a falsehood, I note it and say, "I don't think that's true, but go on, let's assume it is." I note my objection but don't get in the way of their explanation.

Usually what happens is that they have been so stuck arguing on behalf of their moral frame that they haven't bothered to think about the consequences of their proposal in the real world. Your goal is to ask them to describe how their proposal works or doesn't work in the real world and how it does or does not accomplish their stated objectives

This is where you can start suggesting alternatives or challenging assumed knowledge by pointing out things that aren't true and offering facts. You don't challenge their frame, only the assumptions about why their proposed solution should work.

Most people assume that if their moral framework is correct their proposed solution or conclusion must also be correct. We all do this so be humble. When you accept their moral framework, you can now explore whether their proposed solution out of all the various solutions is a good one or if it is the best one. You can also help them explore what the unintended consequences of their proposal might be.

For Instance, with the death penalty, we might ask whether life imprisonment without parole is a valid option. Why do they want the death penalty instead of life without parole? Which is cheaper? Which is more moral? What are all the different ways we might keep someone from killing again? What are all the different ways we might deter potential killers. What does science say works and what doesn't?

When you ask these questions, you are able to challenge the other person's reasoning without them realizing they are being challenged. You aren't debating them, you are asking them to pontificate and share their ideas while you consider whether they are valid or not.

You can ask them to consider alternate proposals and weigh them against their preferred proposal. This is something they probably weren't willing to do before because they were too busy defending their moral framework. They don't have to defend their moral framework anymore, so they are free to consider more effective ways to accomplish their stated objectives. Rather than being an antagonist, you are simply helping them solve their problem effectively.

Their way is one way – but it might not be the best way.

Let's try another example of how we might collaboratively problem solve. Let's talk about Sea World and the captive orca population problem. There are arguments being made that keeping orca is cruel. Ok, I accept that, what should we do about it? Release them? Well, there haven't been any successful releases and no reputable expert suggests doing that. The best funded attempt ran out of money, and the animals starved to death. No one who has read the reports on attempts at release would ever suggest doing that. It's off the table. It would be more humane to euthanize them.

Do we keep them from breeding? How exactly are you planning to keep horny mammals from having sex with each other? Are we going to keep males and females separate until they all die? That seems a bit cruel. Sex is necessary for mental health. Withholding it from otherwise healthy animals is not good for them. (Note: most people don't consider captive animals as being sexual in any way – their knowledge is shallow).

Do we not have them on display? How are we going to get the money to feed them and care for them adequately? The for-profit model ensures they have medical care and food and enrichment activities. The cost of keeping these animals is astronomical and non-profit attempts are well meaning, but the animals ended up dying of starvation when the money ran out.

Again, I'm not arguing the point that keeping orcas is cruel. I have accepted that moral premise. But by asking questions about how exactly we should solve this problem while injecting a dose of reality into the conversation I can challenge the conclusion. At the very least, I've introduced doubt. And doubt it a wonderful thing.

Another example we can discuss is welfare. Let's accept the premise that giving handouts to lazy people is bad. I could argue that people on welfare aren't lazy, but let's accept this premise and yield that point.

What should we do for people who lost their job through a layoff? If someone is sick and has no money and goes to the hospital, should we refuse them service knowing that they will die? What about kids? If their parents have no job, should we allow the kids to starve? It's not their fault their parents are jobless.

When you ask Socratic questions, you yield and accept the moral premise and their goals, then try and figure out how this works in the real world, not the idealized world. If they haven't thought it through, they will have to concede that. If it turns out that they don't have a good reason for the things they think and believe that will become obvious too.

You don't have to openly challenge them. Ask them questions from their starting point and help walk them through the problems and difficulties of actually solving the problem they themselves say they want to solve. When it becomes obvious that their proposed solution isn't a very good one, that's when you start suggesting alternatives that may work better.

If you do this well, you will both end up agreeing on basic principles about what ideally should happen and could happen to help solve the problem.

Assuming you have done your work before hand and assuming your positions are grounded in reality, they should end up agreeing with you. If you haven't thought through your positions before doing this, you will have learned something and had your own thinking challenged as a result, which is also a win.

~~~~~

CHAPTER 7: FREETHOUGHT

Freethought is an effective problem-solving skill. That is why we Humanists encourage people to learn the skill. The problem is that every time we argue to win, we aren't engaging in or encouraging freethought. We are telling people to agree with us and giving them reasons why. That's not freethought, that's argument.

Freethought is a personal practice. To teach it you have to encourage people to think. If they just accept your thinking, they aren't thinking for themselves. To encourage freethought, we first should be civil and respectful. We have to model freethought by being willing to have our own thinking challenged.

Don't do this to win. Do this to learn and model the skills you are trying to teach.

I don't ever enter these conversations to "win." I enter them to genuinely learn. I enter them humbly, I may be wrong and I'm willing to let this person teach me I'm wrong. My willingness to learn I am wrong, is the reason I almost always win.

Because I'm always learning, my knowledge is not superficial. It is deep on many topics and for those that it is not, I acknowledge that fact and seek to learn more.

CHAPTER 8: CONCLUSION

If you are going to argue with a Humanist, make sure you have good factual reasons for holding your opinions, because we aren't going to argue with you. We are going to ask questions to challenge you to see if your reasoning is valid.

We do this to find out whether we should change our minds.

We do this to improve our own thinking, not to win an argument.

Every time we learn and improve our own thinking, we improve our arguments. Our own moral reasoning improves and we become surer of our conclusions.

Do not ever assume you are right. Don't assume you know why the other person thinks the way they do. Don't assume they are evil or insane if they don't agree with you. Ask them questions to find out what they believe.

Most people don't think through their ideas and it will become obvious through questioning if that is the case. By questioning them, you encourage them to think. Telling them they are wrong doesn't do anything productive except make you feel superior.

If your thinking and their thinking has been challenged by a discussion, that's a win.

CHAPTER 9: ABOUT THE AUTHOR:

Jennifer Hancock is a mom, author of The Bully Vaccine, and founder of Humanist Learning Systems. Jennifer is unique in that was raised as a freethinker and is considered one of the top speakers and writers in the world of Humanism today. Her professional background is varied including stints in both the for profit and non-profit sectors. She has served as Director of Volunteer Services for the Los Angeles SPCA, sold international franchise licenses for a biotech firm, was the Manager of Acquisition Group Information for a ½ billion dollar company and served as the executive director for the Humanists of Florida. When she became a mother, she decided to stay at home. But that didn't last long. Shortly after her son was born, she published her first book, The Humanist Approach to Happiness: Practical Wisdom. Her speaking and teaching business coalesced into the founding of Humanist Learning Systems which provides online personal and professional development training in humanistic business management and science based harassment training that actually works.

More Learning from Jennifer Hancock

OTHER BOOKS BY JENNIFER HANCOCK

- The Humanist Approach to Happiness
- Jen Hancock's Handy Humanism Handbook
- The Bully Vaccine
- The Humanist Approach to Grief and Grieving

COURSES TAUGHT BY JENNIFER HANCOCK

- Workplace Bullying for HR professionals
- Living Made Simpler
- An Introduction to Humanism
- Socratic Jujitsu: How to Win Arguments Without Argument
- Why Conflict Resolution Doesn't Work When the Problem is Bullying
- Bridging the Generational Divide: Millennials vs. Boomers
- Ending Harassment and Retaliation in the Workplace
- Why is Change so Hard?
- Principles of Humanistic Management
- 7 Sins of Staff Management
- How to Handle Cranky Customer Problems
- New Manager Orientation
- Humanist Group Leadership Lessons
- Sexual harassment training that works – general

- Sexual harassment training that works – AB 1825
- Stop Bullying in our Workplace – Staff Training
- Sexual Harassment Compliance Training
- No Fear Act training
- Planning for Personal Success!
- Talking to your child about death
- The Bully Vaccine Toolkit
- How to talk to your child's school about bullying
- Why Bullies Bully & How to Stop Them

CONNECT WITH ME ONLINE:
- Twitter: **http://twitter.com/#!/JentheHumanist**
- Facebook: **http://www.facebook.com/JentheHumanist**
- Or sign up for my mailing list: **http://eepurl.com/c3LuI**
- Take a course online: **https://humanistlearning.com**

#####

Printed in Great Britain
by Amazon